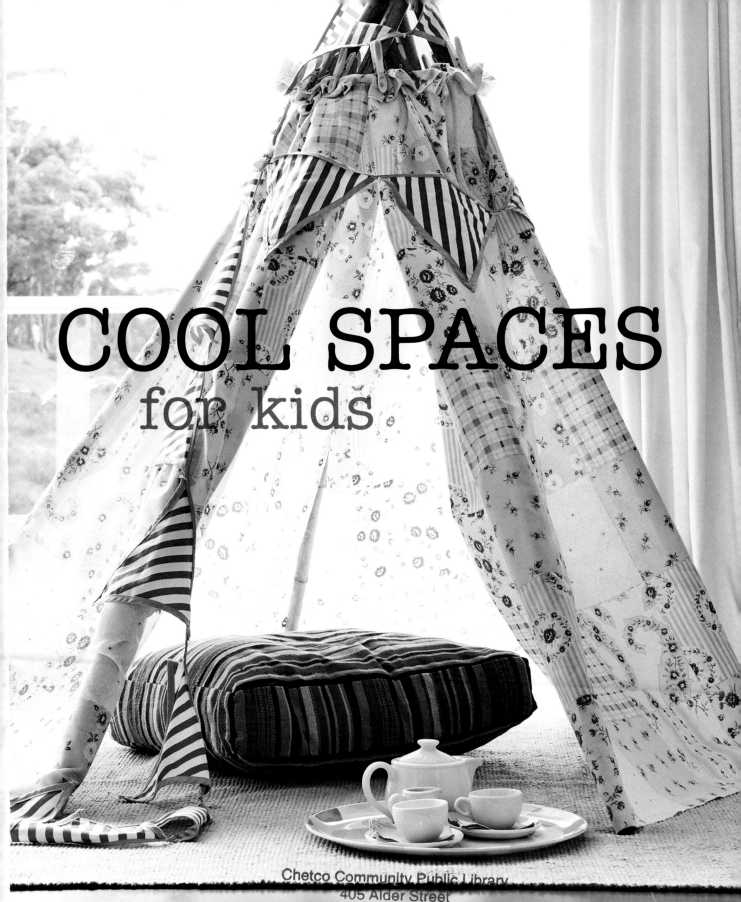

COOL SPACES
for kids

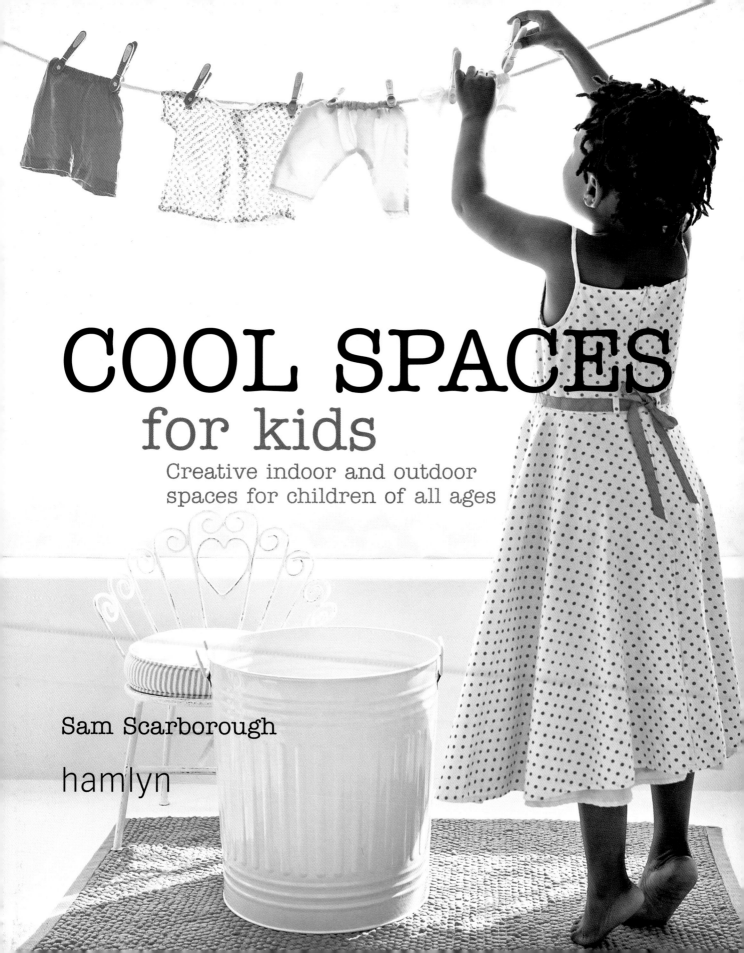

COOL SPACES

for kids

Creative indoor and outdoor
spaces for children of all ages

Sam Scarborough

hamlyn

AAn Hachette UK Company
www.hachette.co.uk

First published in Great Britain in 2009 by
Hamlyn, a division of Octopus Publishing Group Ltd
2-4 Heron Quays, London E14 4JP
www.octopusbooks.co.uk
www.octopusbooksusa.com

Distributed in the U.S. and Canada by Octopus
Books USA:
c/o Hachette Book Group
237 Park Avenue
New York NY 10017

ISBN 978-0-600-61839-3

A CIP catalogue record for this book is available from
the British Library.

Printed and bound in China

10 9 8 7 6 5 4 3 2 1

The Publisher would like to acknowledge
Sam Scarborough for the original design
concept of this work.

contents

introduction

This book is just like a toy cupboard – when you open the doors, a whole new world exists within. Step inside for inspiration and discover how to spot potential in every square inch of your home. Share in the wonder and give your children the freedom to have fun and, quite simply, to play.

All children thrive in a creative environment, so why not indulge them? This book is about transforming everyday areas into fantasy play spaces for children to explore. With 20 'spaces' in total, you will find numerous fantastic ideas for making the most of indoors and out: shared bedrooms, playrooms, garden areas and staircase hideaways. The ideas range from simple hanging storage projects to customizing a wooden garden shed that gives children a miniature home of their own.

There are solutions for activity and workspaces, and everything can be adapted and customized to suit your space and the needs of your children. Very often the simplest ideas are the ones that work best; they can rejuvenate areas that usually go unnoticed, transforming them into magical play spaces. Many of the décor ideas are simple, inexpensive and imaginative, and can change the most basic floor space into an area that provides hours of happy play.

Nowadays, children seem to have so much going on and are constantly entertained and absorbed by television and games that lack imagination. This book will bring the innocent magic of play alive again, encouraging your children to create stimulating games, and allowing you to watch quietly as delightful conversations and ideas come from an improvized tent in the garden, or from behind a fabric puppet theatre hanging in a doorway.

Growing up in a creative house, I am lucky enough to have had a playful childhood. My mother, Annette, was my inspiration in creating the projects for this book and she helped with the making of everything. My daughter, Georgi, tested everything and, through designing and creating for her, I have learned just how much a child can enjoy hours of play with the simplest of toys or games. Hopefully, now, you will be encouraged and inspired to do the same.

① outside spaces

playhouse

There is nothing quite like a mini playhouse in the garden to tempt children away from the television. Convert an old garden shed or buy a new playhouse and have fun creating the ideal space for out-of-doors play.

This project can take a while to complete but you will all have such fun doing it. If converting an old garden shed, begin by making sure the roof doesn't leak so that you can carpet the inside and leave books and toys out there at the end of the day. You can create all sorts of playhouses – perhaps you want to suspend the house on stilts with a ladder leading up to it, for example. This not only makes it more a secretive hideaway, but also creates useful storage space underneath it for bikes, scooters and other big toys. You can also make the place feel like a real home by adding **whirligigs** (see page 16) and window boxes full of vibrant flowers for your children to water. Add **shutters** to the front to encourage imaginative play (see page 14), and a **picnic area** nearby for entertaining family and friends. With such a host of attractions, your children will be busy for hours at a time.

how to add horizontal shutters

Shutters are easily added to a playhouse: simply remove an existing window and attach two horizontal shutters to the frame, fastened using a simple hook. When open, the lower shutter makes a ledge for a shop while the top one doubles as a blackboard.

you will need

Sheet of lightweight wood cut
  to size of window
Tape measure
Pencil
Saw
Gloss paint
Blackboard paint
Paintbrush
Drill
4 hinges with screws
Screwdriver
1 m (40 in) chain
4 large eyehooks
1 latch with screws

1) Measure up and saw the wood to make two shutters that will open horizontally when in position. Paint the outside of each to match the exterior of the playhouse, and paint the inside of the top shutter with blackboard paint. Screw each shutter to the house using two hinges, pre-drilling the holes.

2) Measure two equal-length pieces of chain for the lower shutter and use eyehooks to attach one end of each chain to a top corner of the shutter and the other end to the window frame of the house, pre-drilling the holes. The chains need to be long enough to hold the shutter level when it opens, creating a shop counter.

3) Screw the top part of the latch to the outside of the top shutter; and the bottom part to the outside of the lower one so that both shutters close securely when not in use. Buy a simple latch that allows your children to open and close the shutters themselves and pre-drill the holes.

Make theatre curtains for your playhouse simply by cutting two lengths of lightweight fabric and hemming the short ends of each piece. Thread stretchy curtain cable or elastic through one hem and attach the cable to eyehooks screwed into the window frame inside the house. If you cut the fabric with pinking shears you will not have to edge it.

Point the way to your child's playhouse with a signpost of your own making. Use the template in page 124 to cut a signpost shape from a sheet of hardboard and hammer to a sturdy pole or branch. Paint in a neutral colour and allow to dry before adding names or directions using a permanent marker or darker paint. If you cannot find a suitable pole or branch, attach the sign to the side of the playhouse instead.

outside spaces

you will need

15 cm (6 in) square coloured
  plastic
Ruler
Pen
Craft scissors
Masking tape
Drawing pin
Small, thin bead
Length of thin doweling
Hammer

how to make a whirligig

Whirligigs are delightfully old-fashioned and are a great way to decorate your playhouse. Make a whole row of them for a colourful effect and line them up outside the window or along the edges of the path leading up to the house.

1) Mark and cut an 8 cm (3 in) slit from each corner of the square towards the centre (see below).

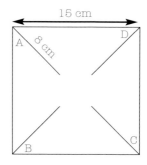

15 cm

A 8 cm   D

B   C

2) Fold each alternate corner into the centre (marked A, B, C, D on diagram above) and anchor all four corners to this centre point using a small piece of masking tape.

3) Carefully push the drawing pin through the middle of the masking tape, thread the bead onto the pointed end of the drawing pin and push the pin into the doweling. Use a hammer if necessary. The bead is essential, as it separates the whirligig from the wood, allowing it to spin more easily.

4) Once secure, peel the masking tape off and you have a whirligig flower to decorate your playhouse garden. Use contrasting colours of plastic and cut shaped edges to the whirligigs to create a different visual effect.

how to make a picnic area

Recycling old tree stumps or logs for a picnic area is an inexpensive and easy project that will provide hours of joy. Paint the wood to give it a fresh, new look and add a tablecloth for tea parties and picnics.

1) Use a hammer and chisel to strip the logs of their outer bark, then sand down any rough surfaces and prepare for painting.

2) Apply two coats of paint, allowing each one to dry completely. Add stripes and spots in different colours for fun.

3) Repeat for the tabletop and hammer the top the table base to secure firmly.

you will need

4 logs for chairs, approx.
   35 cm (13½ in) high
Log for the table, approx.
   57 cm (22½ in) high
Circular piece of wood, approx.
   82 cm (32 in) diameter and
   2.5–5 cm (1–2 in) thick
Hammer
Chisel
Sandpaper
Gloss paint in several colours
Paintbrush
4 long nails
Hammer

Hang a bird feeder on the nearest tree and fill with bird seed so that your children can watch birds eat while they sit quietly in the playhouse.

Update your shutters by adding a decorative wooden trim, or cut heart-shaped peepholes in them for girls and diamond shapes for boys.

Add a flagpole with a pulley rope for attracting Mum's attention. Use plain fabrics and draw symbols for your messages. For example, an apple or a sandwich can be raised when the children are hungry and ready for lunch.

fairy garden

Secret fairy gardens are an absolute delight. Create
the perfect fantasy space with your children
in just a few hours, or start slowly and add to it
over time, letting their imagination grow with it.

This is the perfect project for a summer holiday or following a move to a new house. Let your children explore the garden with new eyes and ask them to choose where they would like their fairy garden to be. They will doubtless opt for a secret corner or bower under a tree in which to create their own little universe complete with twinkly curtains, fairy lights and **wind chimes** (see page 20). This is also a great way to recycle those collections of pretty baubles, beads and buttons that children tend to hoard, and to have fun turning them into hangings for the garden. Find porcelain fairies, merlins and unicorns and give them a new lease of life in this magical world.

Install a water feature, if you like. Children love sprinklers – they make wonderful alternatives to fixed water features and children cannot resist playing in them on hot summer days. A simple birdbath can work too: mosaic the base with flattened glass beads and mirrored tiles for added sparkle.

Once your fairy garden is established, you can add a little pathway to draw you in. Alternatively, children love the fantasy of a wooden bridge that takes them into their secret fairy dell.

Solar-powered lights or candles on poles, lit under supervision, provide the finishing touch and make the garden look especially pretty at dusk.

how to make a bell wind chime

The soft sounds of harmonious bells and chimes add musical charm to a fairy garden and are wonderfully soothing for small children. They are easy to make, and can be hung from a tree or pole at the garden's entrance.

1) Cut a length of string or ribbon for hanging the wind chime, and tie to each end of the twig.

2) Cut a length of string for each bell, thread onto the bell and tie each onto the twig at intervals.

3) Adjust the distances between the strings so that the bells touch each other when the wind blows.

you will need

String or ribbon

Scissors

Length of thin twig or doweling

Bells of different sizes

Make a shimmering mobile by threading shells onto lengths of string and attaching them to a wooden coat hanger or a piece of driftwood. You can make holes in the shells by hammering a screwdriver into the weakest spot. Tie a knot after each shell to prevent it slipping down the string and hide the knot inside the shell if possible. Cut a length of string for hanging the mobile and attach to each end of the coat hanger.

Fairy lanterns are easy to make by tying lengths of ribbon to a garden light. Pop a fairy inside the light holder instead of a candle and you have a 'guardian' to hang near the entrance of your fairy garden, welcoming everyone in.

Recycle old jewellery or visit your local bead shop for pretty beads, crystals and twinkly mirrors to string up on nylon lines. Cut out butterflies from colourful plastic file dividers or any pretty recycled plastic and thread them between the beads and mirrors. The lightness of the nylon makes the butterflies appear to flutter. They look especially beautiful if you hang a whole series of the twinkly strings in a row. Use them to decorate the whole fairy bower or hang them over the entrance.

treehouses

Take the time to build a sturdy treehouse with your children. It does not need to be elaborate, adventurous or complicated – a raised platform with a ladder leading up to it is often sufficient. Finish it off with a flag or a weather vane.

Planning a fantasy space
Spend some time planning with your children. It can be a wonderful bonding experience, so take it slowly and involve them every step of the way. Ask them to draw pictures of their ideal treehouse, and be prepared to adapt your plans! Fill an old toolbox with simple tools for children to use while you build so that they can get involved, too.

Building together Be creative and build hidden trap doors, fixed step ladders for little ones and hanging ladders for older climbers. If it helps you to relax while your children play, add safety netting to the sides of the treehouse or platform. This will also make your children feel more secure in their fantasy world.

Decorate the interior. If you've built a treehouse with a roof you can also get the children to help decorate. Make curtains, fix shutters and window boxes and add floor cushions and blankets to make it cosy. Raid the garage for camping equipment and take up roll-up mattresses and sleeping bags. Older children and teens might like to take up books and music.

Swings and slides Add a zip line for endless abseiling across the garden, tie knotted ropes to branches to shinny up and down or create suspension bridges or walkways. Introduce swings and slides that challenge children of all ages.

Build a treehouse without damaging the tree Use rope along with wooden chocks or wedges for stability and to balance the platform. Recycle the small branches that you may have to remove to make ladders and railings. Keep all the extra logs and bigger tree stumps because children love to learn to balance on them. They'll jump from stump to stump, roll them or simply sit and daydream on them. Line them up in a row, or arrange them in circles: you'll be amazed at how much fun they can be.

Signposts and pulley baskets Build on the excitement by painting signposts and making postboxes. Or donate a picnic basket and show your children how to hoist it up and down on a pulley for lunch supplies or books and other toys.

vegetable garden

Create a space in your garden where your children can experiment with growing herbs and vegetables. It's a wonderfully rewarding project to plan and make together and may even encourage a healthy appetite for more greens at mealtimes.

Most herbs and vegetables thrive in a sunny spot while others, like lettuce, prefer partial sunlight so bear this in mind when you select a site for your vegetable patch. Find a gardening book and look at pictures of vegetables with your children before visiting a nursery.

growing vegetables

Decide what you would like to grow to eat and make a list of your favourites. It's a good idea to have some seedlings that bring fast, eye-catching results like lettuce, spinach and herbs mixed with others that take a little longer to grow and produce. Beans and tomatoes, for example, take longer but are very rewarding and great fun to pick or harvest.

Consult a specialist at the nursery so that you plant the most suitable plants for your vegetable patch. Preparing the ground before planting will ensure that your seedlings are well nourished and grow fast. This is a good thing, because your enthusiastic little gardeners will be watching the progress of growth daily.

Leave a topped-up watering can close by to encourage your children to care for and water their plants regularly. Invite their friends over for the first harvest and celebrate the joy of growing real food together.

how to make a circular vegetable patch

You do not need much space for your first vegetable patch. Start with a small segment each for up to six plant types. If your children really take to 'growing their own' you can consider devoting more of your garden to this activity.

1) Once you have chosen your spot in the garden, hammer the wooden pole into the ground at the centre of your proposed patch. Attach a length of string to the pole and walk away, holding the string in your hand, until you reach the point at which the edge of the vegetable garden should be. Cut the string: this will be your guide for marking the outline of your patch with pebbles or shells in a neat circle. (Walk around the pole in a circle, holding the string taut, and place pebbles at regular intervals at the end of the string).

2) Use the same idea to divide your circular patch into segments. Lay the string on the ground from the pole in the centre to any point on the pebble outline and place shells, bark, pebbles or sticks along the length of the string to divide the circular vegetable patch into segments. (Six dividing lines work well).

3) Prepare each segment in the circle by digging in the compost and watering well. Then plant the seedlings and water the ground gently with a watering can. We planted six types of vegetable (one in each triangle) but you can mix and match as you like.

you will need

Wooden pole

Hammer

String

Scissors

Painted pebbles or cockleshells

Bark and sticks

Spade

Compost (at least enough to cover your surface area to a depth of 5 cm (2 in)

Watering can

Vegetable and herb seedlings

Create a garden in pots in a courtyard or plant a row of pots with sunflowers. Alternatively, you could decorate a wooden trellis with hanging pots on a balcony or deck.

Recycle tins to use as plant holders and decorate them by sticking shells or seeds to the outside. Make use of a very sunny spot such as a windowsill and you'll be surprised how much you can grow.

how to make a scarecrow

Everyone in the family can get involved in making a scarecrow. Little ones can try their hand at stuffing hay into the head and body and choosing buttons for eyes, while the older children are busy digging and planting.

1) Lay the clothes out flat. Slip the short pole through the shirtsleeves and the long pole through the neck opening. Use a good length of string to tie the two poles together securely where they cross over.

2) Stuff the trousers with straw, then tie the bottom of each leg, leaving a little straw sticking out and 'dress' your scarecrow in the trousers. Now stuff the shirt and sleeves with straw.

3) Stuff the stocking with enough straw to make a large round head. Stitch on the buttons for eyes and embroider a nose and mouth. Attach the head to the body of the scarecrow by slipping the open end of the stocking over the top of the longest pole and tying securely with string.

4) Drive the base of the long pole firmly into the ground using a mallet, so that he 'stands up'. Finally, dress your scarecrow with a hat, and he'll be ready to start protecting your new seedlings from birds.

you will need

Old clothes (shirt, trousers, waistcoat, necktie)
Short wooden pole
Long wooden pole
String
Scissors
Straw
Skin-tone stocking
2 large buttons
Embroidery needle and thread
Hat
Mallet

Make a fence for your vegetable garden. Any sticks will do – odd sizes and different thicknesses give it a more rustic look. Simply lay the sticks out on the ground at regular intervals and tie them with string or wire to horizontal sticks top and bottom to hold them all together.

Adapt a regular shopping bag into a handy bag for child-size storing garden tools. Glue a useful pocket to the front for storing seed packets and stitch on some large buttons from which to hang your hand tools.

A great storage idea for all your tools, gardening apron and watering cans is a trellis. Fix it to a wall and add a few large butcher's hooks so that you can hang everything up easily.

garden tent

Fresh air, fun games and living the wild life makes for happy, healthy children, and rarely does a child pass up the chance of camping in the garden. A simple A-frame tent is easy to put up and pack away, and can be used for parties as well as play.

You will be surprised how much use you can get from a basic **garden tent** (see page 32). At the very least, it can provide hours of outdoor fun and fantasy, doubling as a playhouse equipped with dolls and their clothes, beds and toys or teddy bears having a picnic. Or use as a shady haven at parties, and throw in some cushions.

Most children will want to try a 'sleep out' in their tent. For this, you could add some flags, a groundsheet, cushions and a mattress, blankets, lanterns and a picnic basket full of goodies for a midnight feast. Add to the theme by having a barbecue that night and sit around the fire looking at the stars.

how to make an A-frame garden tent

This is one of the easiest structures to make and provides hours of fun wherever you go. It's known as the seven-pole tent and is literally made with rope, a long sheet of fabric and seven poles.

1) Use rope to tie the poles together to make a basic frame (see below). Stabilize the two ends by making four string guy ropes and attach two to each apex of the frame, then fix into the ground using tent pegs.

2) Drape your fabric over the structure and secure it into place around the poles using laundry pegs. Cushions, sleeping bags and blankets can also be used to 'hold' the fabric down at the sides – just tuck the fabric underneath them inside the tent.

you will need

7 wooden or bamboo poles of
  equal length
Rope
String
4 tent pegs
Hammer
Long sheet of fabric
Laundry pegs

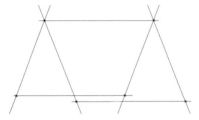

Buy a ready-made gazebo and shorten the
legs to make it more cosy for children. Then
customize with a fabric of your colour choice:
simply sew the fabric over the existing covering
and add some triangular bunting detail along
each side at the top (see page 54 for
instructions on how to make triangular flags).

favourite spaces

interactive wall mural

A child's play space should be as engaging and multifaceted as possible. This project takes the traditional wall mural into a new dimension by making it interactive, tactile and as close to the real thing as possible.

The idea of painting a mural this size might seem daunting, but all of the elements are simple and it will be sure to delight your child when finished, so do give it a try. The trick is to break the mural down into sections and complete each one in turn (see pages 40–41).

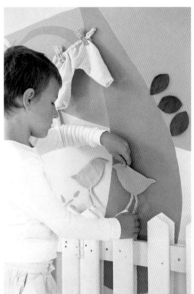

stimulating imagination

Colourful murals stimulate a child's imagination, and this example offers a detailed and interactive design. Choose a subject that particularly appeals to your child – toy shops, children's clothing stores, trains and farmyards all make great subjects and can be adapted in many ways to suit the age group or a theme – let your imagination go and have fun.

Children will happily pretend to play with a cat or dog, or have the sense of a tree in their house. You could even add some bird music or add to the idea of living in a neighbourhood by having your own street name and number incorporated into your design.

A good, old-fashioned projector is a great way to transfer your design onto a wall. If this is not an option for you, you can draw your mural onto tracing paper and divide it into a grid before copying it onto the wall section by section.

how to make an interactive wall mural

There are countless possible themes for a wall mural: this one shows a simple street scene. Among the 'interactive' elements are window shutters, a picket fence, a postbox and felt birds and animals.

you will need

Overhead projector or tracing
  paper
Pencil
Ruler
Chalk
Washable satin-sheen paint in
  a range of colours
Paintbrushes
Masking tape
Permanent marker
Ready-made picket fence
  (180 cm or 70⅞ in is a
  standard size)
Circular saw or handsaw
Drill
2 hinges with screws
Latch with screws
Masonry screws
Rawlplugs
Screwdriver
Ready-made postbox with hook
Nail
Hammer
Crystal doorknob
All-purpose glue
2 ready-made window shutters
2 eyehooks

2 hemmed curtains to fit
  window
Length of curtain cable to fit
  window
20 cm (8 in) hook-and-loop
  fastener
Round LED camping light
Sealant
25 cm (10 in) black fabric
2 felt squares in different
  colours, approx. 21 cm (8½ in)
Scissors

1) Choose your scene and draw it up on transparent projector paper. Project onto the wall and adjust until you are happy with the proportions (you will not be able to fit the whole image on the projector at once). Trace your outline in chalk, ready for painting. Repeat this process as many times as is needed across the wall space to complete the outline.

2) If you don't have access to a projector, draw your outline on tracing paper and then, using a pencil and ruler, draw a grid over the whole picture. A useful guide for grid size: 5 cm (2 in) tracing-paper grid squares correspond to a 50 cm (20 in)

square on the wall. Copy your grid onto your wall using a long ruler and chalk. Now copy the image that fits into each square of your grid.

3) Paint your mural from left to right, working on the outlines first. Keep masking tape handy for painting straight lines, and tidy up any untidy outlines using a permanent marker.

4) Use a saw to cut the picket fence into three sections: one piece to form the gate and two to make the fence either side. Screw two hinges to one side of the gate and attach this to one section of picket fence,

pre-drilling the holes first. Lay all sections on the floor, with the gate in place, and mark screw holes for the latch on the gate section and where it should meet the remaining section of picket fence. Attach the latch with screws, again pre-drilling the holes. Once complete and working correctly, screw the single piece of picket fence to the wall first, then line up the gate section and screw this into the wall with the masonry screws. Pre-drill the holes for this.

5) Decide where to hang the postbox, hammer a nail into the wall and hang the box securely from its hook. Glue the crystal knob to the front door and paint your house number onto it. Add the street name too, if you like, so that your child learns to recognize it.

6) Screw the window shutters into position and screw in the eyehooks (out of sight if possible). Pre-drill all of the holes. Thread the curtain cable through the hems of both curtains and attach the curtain cable to the eyehooks.

7) Mark the position of the sun and paint it in. Cut a strip of hook-and-loop fastener and glue one half at the centre of the sun. Attach the corresponding strip to the back of the LED light and stick in place. (Most camping lights switch on when touched.)

8) Seal the wall with a recommended sealant so that it's fully washable and protected from mishaps with pens or any other creative additions.

9) To complete the wall mural, glue on hook-and-loop fasteners for a cat (cut from the black fabric), leaves, flowers, birds and any other animals or features you might want to add (cut from felt).

kiddies' corner

If you are short of space, there are still countless stylish ideas for a play corner for anywhere in the home. Set aside a small area in the room you use most that gives your children somewhere to settle in an adult zone.

Younger children will love easy access to a mini table space they can call their own and where they can leave their artwork and return to it a few hours later. Find chairs to match: look out for antique miniature chairs, retro chair sets or plain wooden ones that can be painted in a colour that blends with your scheme. If they are made from brightly coloured plastic that doesn't complement your décor, simply make **chair covers** for them in hardwearing denim (see page 44).

Perfect for older children are two simple foam blocks upholstered in removable fabric slipcovers and designed to fit neatly under a simple

desk structure. Space saving and discreet, the whole unit can be coordinated to blend with any style. Two box-like chairs with hinged lids could also be constructed out of wood, providing useful storage underneath.

Give your kiddies' corner a creative element by adding an **art wall** (see page 47 or a blackboard. Keep supplies of chalk near the board, and various other art materials at the ready. Consider introducing a decorative screen with storage pockets, where everything is visible at a glance and easy to reach. Finally, paint the tops of **storage boxes** with blackboard paint for a fun twist (see page 46).

how to make a chair cover

If you cannot bear to have plastic chairs in your living room, but want to have a special kiddies' corner, cover the chairs with easy-care denim slipcovers. Add a storage pocket for each child's favourite pens, papers, toys and treasures.

you will need

Newspaper
Tailor's chalk
Scissors
Approx. 150 x 150 cm
    (60 x 60 in) denim fabric
Tape measure
Dressmaker's pins
Sewing needle and matching
    thread
Sewing machine and matching
    thread

favourite spaces

1) There are various small chairs for children. This pattern is designed for a standard plastic chair without armrests, but can easily be adapted to suit a smaller wooden one or other shape. Start by creating a pattern from newspaper using the shapes and measurements given (see below).

2) You need to cut two pieces of fabric for the sides of the chair cover. Make a template for this by attaching a sheet of newspaper to one side of your chair and drawing its outline using tailor's chalk (see Diagram A below). Cut two pieces from the fabric, making sure you flip the template for one of them, and adding a 1 cm (½ in) seam allowance.

3) The back, front and seat of the chair are made from one single strip of fabric. Make another template, using your measurements for the side panels as a guide. Measure the required length and width, adding 1 cm (½ in) to the width where the seat meets the back of the chair (see Diagram B for how this works). This slightly extended shape is designed to cope with the extra width needed for the slight indent in the seat of the chair. Now cut this piece from the fabric, adding a 1 cm (½ in) seam allowance.

4) Pin the two side panels to the main piece, right sides together, and tack by hand. Machine-sew the seams together, finishing them off securely. Turn inside out and hem the base. Iron and fit.

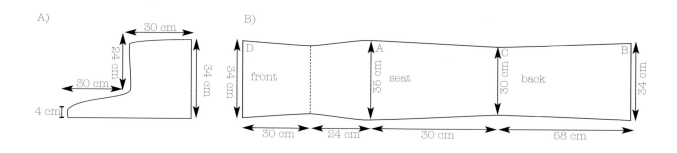

how to make a blackboard storage box

Storage boxes make the best space savers in small places, even more so if they have castors, which make them easy to move from room to room. This version doubles up as a blackboard and pull-along play toy for added fun.

1) Make sure the top of the storage box is smooth and free of dust. Prepare the lid by sticking masking tape around the top edges to protect the sides of the box from drips of paint. Paint the lid with at least two coats of blackboard paint. When dry, carefully peel off the masking tape, and touch up if necessary.

2) Add castors if your box doesn't have wheels, pre-drilling the holes and screwing in place (see below). To add a rope handle, drill a hole in one short side of the box, thread the rope through the hole and tie a knot on the inside of the box to secure it.

you will need
Ready-made storage box
Masking tape
Blackboard paint
Paintbrush
4 lockable castors with screws
Drill
Rope

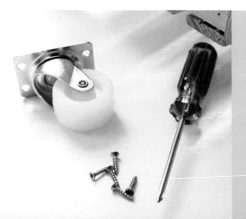

When adding castors to the bottom of a storage box, it is best to place them 2 cm (¾ in) in from the edges.

how to make a creative 'art wall'

Drawing and painting activities encourage children to express themselves. Ideal for a compact space, this mini art station, combines paper 'on tap' with handy pots for brushes, crayons, pencils and scissors and a small shelf for storing art materials during bursts of creativity.

1) Paint the wood backing and the wooden strip. Attach the wooden strip near the bottom of the wood backing to form a shelf. Screw from the back and pre-drill the holes. (You could glue the strip to the board, depending on size and weight.)

2) Attach the roll of paper and its holder, with the screws supplied, pre-drilling the holes first.

3) At the bottom of the board, just above the shelf, attach a length of elastic to tuck the end of the paper into, to prevent it from curling up. Drill holes into the board (further apart than the width of the paper), thread the elastic through the holes and tie at the back.

4) Hammer the beakers into place. This example has three along the top of the board and one at the bottom. Attach the board to the wall using masonry screws and pre-drilling the holes.

you will need
100 x 75 cm (40 x 30 in) wood backing
Wooden strip
Eggshell paint
Paintbrush
Drill
2 screws
Screwdriver
Roll of paper, with holder and screws
Thin elastic
4 coloured beakers
4 nails
Hammer
4 masonry screws
4 rawlplugs

Children need space for all creative projects so it's best to create a corner where they can paint and have good fun. Wipe-clean surfaces are essential – sealed fabric cloths in bright patterns are ideal.

Try covering the floor in interlinking pieces of rubber matting or linoleum. As well as protecting the floor, this is a great way to introduce a colour to hold the whole scheme together.

a bedroom for boys

Not many boys would resist having their own private den – some might like the idea of sharing with a brother, especially if each boy has his own personal zone and individualized play space decorated in his choice of style and colour.

The easiest way to create zones in a room shared by more than one boy is through flooring and storage. Each can be chosen to reflect individual taste and will hold together well if there is a common colour or theme.

sharing a bedroom

Features in a shared room can include mobiles and blackboard walls (see pages 55 and 56). The former can soften the boyish look of a room and can be hung wherever the child would like to lie and watch them. The latter create a personal art zone, where doodles can be changed at will, or on which to display after-school activity schedules.

A rug can become a dedicated space for each boy to own, play on and leave his toys. You can use triangular **name flags** to designate an area and **framed name** letters to give each child a sense of identity (see pages 54 and 57). Personalize sturdy **toy boxes** for growing collections of Lego, dressing-up kit, sports equipment or anything that needs a home at the end of the day. A hammock is a great storage idea – ideal for balls and soft toys. Most homeware stores sell hammocks in striking colours, with bright stripes or spots.

how to personalize a toy box

This box is likely to take quite a bit of wear if kept in a little boy's bedroom or the playroom. Choose a sturdy box that's big enough to hold everything from hockey sticks and footballs to train tracks.

1) Make a stencil of the initial letter of your child's name by drawing the capital letter in a style and size of your choice on the thin card or acetate and cut out carefully using the craft knife. (You can also scan and print or photocopy capital letters from books and magazines onto card or acetate, enlarging them to any size you want.)

2) Position the child's initial on the box and temporarily fix it down with reusable adhesive so that it can be removed after spraying. Spray-paint the letter and leave it for at least 20 minutes before removing the stencil, allowing it to dry thoroughly.

you will need

Thin card or acetate
Pencil
Ruler
Craft knife
Wooden or metal box
Reusable adhesive
Spray paint

Cover shoe boxes with fabric, wallpaper or wrapping paper in spots, stripes or whatever suits the décor to make another great bedroom storage device. Lay the shoe box on the fabric or paper and cut out around the edges, leaving a little extra to fold over. Prepare the box with double-sided tape and secure the fabric to it. Use pinking shears to prevent the edges fraying and make sure you pull the fabric tight when you glue it down to prevent it forming folds of trapped air.

how to make a name flag

Name flags are easy to hang anywhere – over a headboard, on a door, at the foot of a bed or even on the wall. They are a great way of identifying a sense of ownership over an area in shared bedrooms.

you will need

Fabric for flags
Tape measure
Tailor's chalk
Sharp scissors
Dressmaker's pins
Sewing machine and matching
    thread
Fabric for letters
Embroidery needle and thread
Iron
Bias binding
2 drawing pins or small nails
Hammer

1) You need the right number of fabric triangles to spell your child's name – two for each letter. The length of the name and the space in which it must fit will determine the size of these triangles. It is a good idea to experiment with newspaper until you arrive at a size that works. (The triangles used here are 20 cm (8 in) high and 15 cm (6 in) wide.)

2) Measure and cut two triangles per flag. Cut each letter of your child's name from your chosen fabric, using pinking shears and stitch them on by hand with embroidery thread: blanket stitch and running stitch both look good and add detail, particularly if you use thread of a contrasting colour. Alternatively, with your sewing machine, you can edge each letter with satin stitch and then glue the letters to the triangles.

3) Pin the triangles right sides together. Machine-stitch the two edges that form the V-shape of the triangle. Use sharp scissors to make short snips in the raw edge of the sewn sides at regular intervals of about 1 cm (½ in) (taking care not to snip the stitching as well). This makes it easier to achieve a smooth edge when turning the triangles right sides out. Iron each triangle flat.

4) Attach each completed triangle to the bias binding. Simply slip the triangle into the bias and machine-stitch it closed. The slight stretch in bias binding allows the triangles to hang in a slight curve on a headboard as here.

5) Attach the name flags to your child's headboard using drawing pins or small nails. (If you want to attach them to a wall, you'll need to use masonry nails.)

how to make an easy mobile

Many boys go through a phase of creating intricate model aircraft, trains, boats, cars – even dinosaurs. By making them into mobiles, you can have them on display permanently, while keeping the bedroom shelves free of excess clutter.

1) Fold the denim fabric in half lengthways, right sides together, and lay the coat hanger on top. Draw around the shape of the coat hanger using tailor's chalk, adding a 2 cm (¾ in) seam allowance. Cut out the denim shape and use this as a template to cut the same shape from the batting.

2) Lay the batting on top of the denim fabric (still right sides together) and pin together. Machine-sew around the edges, leaving a small opening for the coat hanger hook. Turn inside out and slip over the coat hanger, pushing the hook between your sewing stitches.

3) Attach one end of the shoelace to the aircraft with glue (or thread it through a handy hole and knot beneath) and staple the other end to the underside of the coat hanger. Now fold the open seams inwards and hand-stitch the opening to close.

4) Screw the cup hook into the ceiling. Attach a suitable length of fishing line to the hook of the coat hanger hook and tie it onto the hook in the ceiling.

you will need

25 cm (10 inches) denim fabric
Wooden coat hanger
Tailor's chalk
Scissors
25 cm (10 inches) batting
Dressmaker's pins
Sewing machine and matching thread
Shoelace or length of ribbon
Model aircraft
All-purpose glue
Staple gun
Needle and thread
Cup hook
Fishing line

Mobiles can be made in many ways: tie two pieces of wire with fishing line to form a cross shape and use pliers to curl up each end decoratively. The design allows you to hang a plane from each of the curled ends. Or use two interesting pieces of driftwood or recycled doweling to create the cross frame, tying them together in the same way. If you're hanging fighter planes, use camouflage fabric to cover the hanger and a green or brown ribbon to hang it.

how to make a blackboard wall

An excellent way of defining zones in a shared bedroom, a blackboard does not have to be black – any dark colour works well. Boys will love leaving a drawing up for days, changing it here and there at whim.

you will need

Tape measure

Pencil

Spirit level

Masking tape

Thin card

1 litre (1¾ pint) blackboard
  paint

Paintbrush

Chalk

Paint roller and tray

1) Mark the preferred height of your blackboard on the wall by measuring from the floor upwards at 20 cm (8 in) intervals. A spirit level is handy tool if you have one, as not all skirting boards are level. Use your markings as a guide to outline the board area with masking tape.

2) Make card trains for your design using the templates on page 122, and use masking tape to position them on the top line of the board area. Trace around each one in pencil. Remove the templates and fill in with blackboard paint using the paintbrush, painting in one direction only to avoid smudging. (Once dry, you can add in chalk-drawn windows for the carriages and train engine.)

3) Now fill in the board area using the paint roller and tray. Two coats of paint are usually recommended. Allow to dry thoroughly before removing the masking tape and touch up any ragged edges.

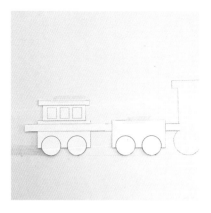

Buy basic picture frames and use each to hold a letter of your child's name. Simply cut each letter from fabric using pinking shears or scissors and glue or sew to a contrasting background fabric. Glue the background fabric to a piece of card, place inside the frame and affix firmly. Hang each one with a picture hook to spell your child's name.

You can use any colour PVA paint to create a drawing area on a wall and the shape or stencil can be customized to suit the theme of the room. A long board with two train templates (each possibly facing a different direction) is a good idea for two boys who share a room. Magnetic paint is a fun alternative to traditional blackboard paint and can be used along an entire wall in a bedroom, playroom or kitchen, doubling up as an art display area.

A blackboard wall can be quite scary in the dark, so it's a good idea to stick glow-in-the-dark stars to the wall above the blackboard paint or onto each train carriage. A silhouette of a train or recognizable shape also helps to make the area more familiar in the dark.

music room

Set up a music corner with plenty of chairs, a soft rug and possibly some blankets on the walls for soundproofing. A range of 'musical instruments', from tin cans filled with stones to violins, will not only introduce the children to rhythm and sounds but can also be very theraputic for some.

Decorate Make this corner a welcoming area with plenty of space and chairs for friends who want to join in. Hang some pictures on the walls, add a beanbag or two and gather together any instruments you've collected over the years: bells, tambourines, shaking sticks, maracas, recorders, a trumpet – even a guitar or violin.

Drummers and percussionists Installing a drum in one corner will give the area an instant 'band' feeling. Floor drums or marimbas are also great for children of all ages.

Make a bottle orchestra Hang up a row of glass jars or bottles with different volumes of water inside them (the more water in the bottle, the higher the note). Or try hanging up a row of aluminium pipes or tubes with holes in them: different lengths to produce a variety of sounds. Add a paint tin lid to the row and you have an instant gong.

Homemade instruments
Homemade versions are easy to find: pots and pans make great 'drums' or cymbals and gongs (use rulers or long wooden pens for drumsticks). Bells can be attached to a ribbon and tied to wrists or ankles.

Make shakers Easy to make and to 'play', shakers are the perfect instruments for the youngest members of the 'band'. Fill a dry water bottle with beans, lentils or pasta, close the lid and give to your child to play by holding the narrow neck area and shaking it.

Band practice Children who take part in bands at school will love having a place to practise their music, so that they can keep time and stay in tune. Hang blankets on the walls to absorb sound if your neighbours can hear you!

Keep a record Easily done on a portable music system or video camera, recording these precious moments will give your children a confidence boost. Record every time they play, allowing them to create their own scores over a number of sessions.

a bedroom for girls

The best space saver in a shared room is bunk beds. Reorganize the shared bedroom and create unique areas for each child within the room. Paint wall murals, provide shelving for each girl's photos, precious collections or books, and personalize storage for toys.

Every child needs her own special space in a shared bedroom and if girls are sleeping in bunk beds each will need her own cupboards, play areas and storage.

sharing a room

The easiest solution to creating individual spaces is to use wall murals to designate a 'corner' for each girl, so that she feels that her side of the room is decorated especially for her (see page 64).

Add box shelving on the walls for each girl's personal collections of fairies, dolls and books. This will also save on floor space. Create **mini galleries** of the girls' paintings and pictures, either putting them in pretty frames, printing them onto canvas or block mounting them (see page 66).

When it comes to choosing furniture, there are many new, modular furniture designs with cupboards or desks underneath bunk beds and other clever storage configurations. Alternatively, you could give vintage furniture a new lease of life with a fresh coat of paint.

how to paint a wall mural

A wall mural is a quick and easy way of personalizing a corner of a shared bedroom. Involve your girls in deciding whether to have the same frieze in different colours, or a different design each, but in the same colour.

1) Decide on a simple design for your frieze and make paper templates for the shapes required (see pages 122–125). It is easiest to paint a frieze in a line, neatly contained within a border. Start by measuring and marking the desired position of your border in pencil, using a long ruler. If you have a spirit level handy, use it to check that everything is level. Use masking tape to make sure that your lines are crisp and straight.

2) Draw in your stencil pattern, fixing the template in position using reusable adhesive. Once this is complete, begin painting, starting with the borders. It is wise to work in one direction only and to let each section dry before moving on. Once the borders are complete, fill in the stencilled pattern. Only when everything is dry should you remove the masking tape.

you will need

Paper
Pencil
Scissors
Long ruler
Spirit level
Masking tape
Reusable adhesive
Acrylic PVA paint
Paintbrush

Apply your painting skills to the bedroom door. This makes an ideal place for painting a measuring chart. Alternatively each child could have a growth chart on her own cupboard door. Begin by drawing a line down the centre of the door and use a black pen to mark off the measurements. Then have fun drawing your own floral design freehand in pencil, before filling it in with acrylics.

For **extra sparkle**, add glitter paint or glow-in-the-dark paint to wall murals. Pearl, silver or metallic paints also catch the light and look pretty in a girly bedroom. Alternatively, visit your nearest craft shop and decorate your mural with pretty papers, stickers or stamp effects.

▶ 150

how to make an art gallery wall

Preserve your girls' precious art by creating a mini gallery. Look out for inexpensive frames of similar sizes and paint them all the same pale colour. Select a few pieces to have printed onto canvas and stapled to frames for contrast.

you will need

Selection of framed and
  canvas works
Tape measure
Pencil
Picture hooks with pins
Hammer
Newspaper
Scissors
Ruler

1) Lay out all your works on the floor and swap them around until you are happy with the arrangement. Measure the collective height of all the pictures and transfer this measurement to the wall. It is best to avoid hanging pictures lower than 70 cm (28 in) from the floor, to prevent them getting damaged.

2) Begin by hanging the pictures in the middle, then work upwards and downwards. If you don't feel confident about getting the arrangement right, trace each work on newspaper, cut out and tack to the wall. Mark the outline of each with a pencil. Remove from the wall, stand back and check that all the lines are straight. If not, use a ruler to line them up neatly.

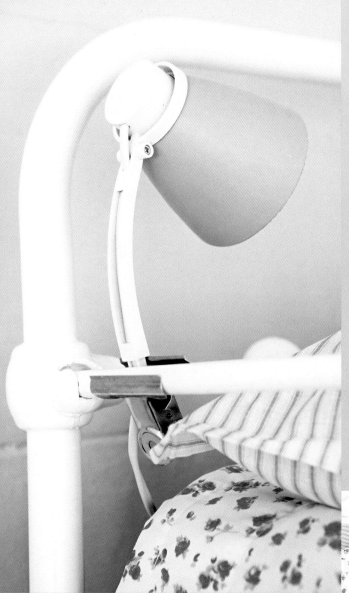

Attach individual nightlights or reading lamps to headboards, allowing each child to read on her own. You can even personalize light-switch panels for each child. Alternatively, personalize lampshades by adding buttons, ribbons or felt flowers and shapes.

Storage is always a challenge in shared bedrooms and these pockets, fixed with tab tops to the end of a bed, offer a clever solution. Decorate the pockets with hearts, flowers or even initials, and customize each one so that it is the right size for a favourite toy.

③ activity spaces

foldaway cupboard

Play cupboards are ingenious all-in-one spaces, providing opportunities for imaginative play. The themes to use are endless and the best bit is that you can close the doors on it all at the end of the day.

For girls you might make a dressing room, complete with torch lights, a round a mirror, makeup drawers, dressing-up clothes, racks for shoes and hooks for bags. Boys might prefer a workshop, complete with workbench, tool box, hooks for tools, spare wood and doweling to hammer and saw. Screws, nails, drawing pins and other small pieces can be stored in upside-down jam jars or baby food jars. Others ideas include a mini hospital, a playschool and a shop, complete with baskets of fruits and vegetables, weighing scales, a till and hooks for paper bags.

Start with a blank canvas: an empty cupboard. Design and custom-make the interior to suit whatever purpose you have in mind. This example has a fitted kitchen, complete with shelving, a kitchen counter and household appliances, such as a microwave, a kettle, a mixer and a washing machine. Decorate and paint inside and out, then get to work on the doors, giving them as many functions as possible. Here, the cupboard doors have bunk beds for dolls on one side and an ironing board fixed to the other. There are hooks, rails and a washing line for all manner of domestic activities. Decorate the outside of the cupboard, too, painting the doors and adding fairy lights.

how to make a foldaway cupboard

Use an existing bookshelf or custom-make a unit to fit any cupboard you like, and adapt it to your child's needs. Once you have the basic structure in place, you can have fun painting, decorating and adding the finer details.

you will need

Cupboard
Shelving
Eggshell paint
Paintbrushes
Selection of decorative papers
   and fabrics, including pretty
   giftwrap and wallpaper
Cork pin board
Double-sided tape
Clothes hooks
Washing line and pegs
Wooden boxes
Drill
Screws
Screwdriver
Netting
Mirror

1) Install the shelving and basic interior structure first and paint it. When dry you can add the fun, decorative touches: wallpaper on the walls; pretty giftwrap to line behind the shelves; and coloured paper or fabric to line the cupboard – whatever you fancy. Once complete, paint the floor.

2) Add any features you like. Attach a cork pin board to the inside of one door, using double-sided tape. Add a knob or hook to the board by screwing through the board and into the cupboard door to make a firm fixture for hanging the ironing board. Add hooks for tutus and dressing-up outfits on the right-hand door and another row of hooks inside the cupboard for kitchen utensils and dishcloths. Put up a washing line (string, ribbon or stretchy line all work well) and pegs.

3) Screw the two wooden boxes to the inside of the other door to make bunk beds and screw in a hook centrally above the top bunk. Use this to drape a mosquito net or coronet over the beds. Finally, add a mirror – make one up with foil and a frame if you don't have one small enough to fit the door.

String up an easy-to-reach washing line, and provide brightly coloured pegs. Two recycled wooden boxes make perfect bunk beds. Drape a lacy fabric or netting over one to make the bed more cosy for a dolly.

Turn a bookshelf into a dolls' house by adding vertical struts for walls, cutting out windows with a jigsaw and adding a staircase and balcony (thick wooden skewers or ice lolly sticks are really useful for this).

play mats

You can make play mats for all kinds of play, simply let your imagination run wild. Incorporate games into your designs for rainy-day play or bag the mats up to take out with you on picnic trips and holidays.

All young children love play mats. Babies and toddlers enjoy having a soft, warm surface to roll about and play on in the nursery, and these can be made very effectively from sheets of foam rubber cut into interesting shapes or from soft, fleecy fabrics.

Older children will entertain themselves for hours with mats that incorporate all manner of games and activities. Use a groundsheet to make a **waterproof racetrack** embellished with fabric racing cars and any scenery your child wants to 'drive' through on his imaginary journeys (see page 78). Alternatively incorporate a farmyard

scene into your design. Using waterproof fabric in this way means that you can spread the mat on damp grass and change nappies more comfortably when out and about. Layering batting within the mat makes it lovely and soft to sit on: you'll be surprised at how much use you get from it.

Other games you could incorporate into play mats are **hopscotch** (see page 80), snakes and ladders and noughts and crosses. If you are likely to take the mats with you on day trips and holidays, make drawstring bags to store them in to keep them clean and tidy.

how to make a waterproof racetrack groundsheet

Children will love to play on this mat. As well as cars, you could incorporate petrol stations, tall buildings, trees, houses, garages, lakes, tunnels and mountains into your design. Use fabric scraps and satin-stitch around the edges to finish off neatly.

you will need

150 x 170 cm (59 x 67 in) dark denim fabric, plus scraps

Tape measure

Scissors

Sewing machine and matching thread

100 x 150 cm (39 x 59 in) light denim fabric

Dressmaker's pins

150 x 150 cm (59 x 59 in) waterproof fabric

150 x 150 cm (59 x 59 in) batting

Needle and thread

1) Cut a 150 cm (59 in) square from the dark denim, and two strips measuring 150 x 10 cm (59 x 4 in) each. Fold each of the two long strips in half down the length, right sides together, and stitch to form ties for the finished mat. Turn right side out and iron flat, with the seam at the back.

2) Cut a track from the light denim fabric, and cut a car shape from the dark denim scrap. Position the car on the track and sew into place. Now pin the track onto the denim background and sew together.

3) To assemble the mat, place the car-track fabric right side up on a table, lay the waterproof fabric on top of it, followed by the batting. Pin and tack all three layers together, leaving an opening of 35 cm (14 in) along one side. Machine-sew along the edges and edge the fabric for extra strength.

4) Turn the mat right sides out and position the ends of the ties in the opening before stitching together. Stitch a neat border around the whole groundsheet approximately 3 cm (1 in) from the edges.

5) In order to keep all of the layers in place, you need to hand-sew them at regular intervals, just as you would a traditional quilt, (see below). When storing the mat, roll it up with the car track on the inside and tie the bundle together with the two ties.

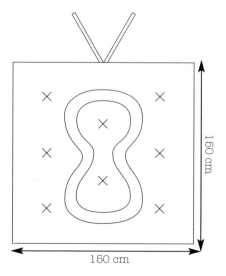

150 cm

150 cm

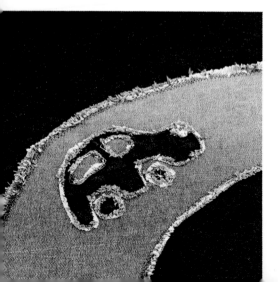

Puzzle floor mats are extremely useful, as they are lightweight and easy to move around and keep little ones warm if they are playing on the floor. Ask your nearest foam shop to cut 'puzzle' pieces from 3-cm (1-in) thick foam rubber.

how to make a hopscotch mat

Easy to enjoy at home or to roll up and take to the park to play with friends or to pack in the car when going on holiday, this inexpensive and lightweight mat will provide children with hours of joy.

you will need

110 x 150 cm (44 x 60 in)
   hessian fabric
Tape measure
Tailor's chalk
5 m (5 yd) white tape, approx.
   5 cm (2½ in) wide
Scissors
Fabric glue
Paper
Pencil
Dressmaker's pins
3 squares coloured felt,
   approx. 21 cm (8½ in) each
15 cm (6 in) square fabric
   scrap
Needle and matching thread
Packet of dried beans or lentils

1) Measure and mark each 'hopscotch' box onto the hessian fabric using tailor's chalk. The boxes here are 30 cm (12 in) square.

2) Use the white tape to outline the boxes, making each one from a single strip of tape and folding it at right angles at the corners. Glue the tape into position.

3) Make a paper template for each of the numbers from 1 to 10, each no smaller than 10 cm (4 in), pin each template to coloured felt and cut out. Glue each number to the centre of a hopscotch square. (They can also be stitched down using a sewing machine.)

4) Make a beanbag from the square scrap of fabric. Cut it in half and stitch the two rectangles, right sides together, along three sides. Turn right sides out and stuff with dried beans or lentils. Stitch the remaining side neatly.

baking and shop

Little chefs always benefit from a kitchen space in which to create their own mixtures, so why not make a tabletop structure that can be moved around and cleaned easily? Design it to double up as a shop counter.

Keep an eye out for any small cupboard that you could turn into a **mini bakery** (see page 84). Perhaps you can adapt it by adding a slim bookshelf to make the cupboard into a dresser. Decorate the doors and shelves with paper, paint, fabric or ribbon and lace – anything that comes to hand. Make a banner for your mini bakery by sewing cut outs of cakes and cookies onto a fabric backdrop. You can also add cup hooks to the side of the table for dishcloths, oven gloves and aprons.

If you house the cupboard in your kitchen, you could also make a toddler step for your child, so that he can reach all of the ingredients in your store cupboards and even get to the sink to help with washing up.

The same space could work as a shop – sew fabric fruit cut outs or any other products onto a banner. Alternatively, you could choose a name for the shop, cut it out in felt and glue it onto your banner. Add baskets, bags, some play money and you're in business.

how to make a mini bakery

The idea here is to make a wooden banner that you can fix to a small table, cupboard or dresser. Children can then use the top of the cupboard as a work surface or, with a change of banner, a shop counter.

1) Cut cupcake and cookie shapes from the scraps of fabric and sew them onto the length of white fabric to form a banner.

2) Hem the short ends of the banner, leaving just enough room to thread through a length of doweling. Make sure the casing fits snugly over the doweling to prevent the banner slipping down.

3) Measure your banner width and drill two holes in your square piece of wood for the opposite ends of the doweling. Glue these in for extra strength.

you will need

Fabric scraps
Scissors
Length of white fabric
Sewing machine and matching
  thread
2 equal lengths of thin
  doweling
Square piece of wood (slightly
  smaller than the work
  surface)
Drill
Wood glue

activity spaces

Children will find endless uses for these duck steps: in the bathroom for cleaning teeth, in the kitchen so that they can reach the store cupboards and in their bedrooms so that they can get things down from their shelves. Use the template on page 125 to draw a duck shape on some paper and cut two ducks from a sheet of wood using a jigsaw. Screw one duck to each end of a wooden board to make the step. Seal the screw holes with wood filler before painting.

hanging spaces

Children readily absorb themselves in imaginary play, building a variety of houses, hangars and hideouts using every blanket, cushion and box available. Reinvent the space under a staircase, in a doorway or beneath the dining room for hours of playtime fun.

The space under a staircase is hugely appealing to all children. It is cosy and compact and right in the middle of the home, so why not make use of this space to create a fantastic playhouse together? Whatever your theme, having decided on the furniture, toys and decorations to include, you can complete the 'space' with a similarly themed fabric drape or hanging. The hanging can just as easily hang in a doorway for half a day's play. Ideas for themes include a **puppet theatre**, **sailboat house** and an **under-the-table house** (see pages 88, 89 and 90).

All three projects are really simple to make. There are even short cuts to take if your children want to see an instant result: improvize by using glue instead of machine-stitching, or use felt instead of fabric and cut with pinking shears to prevent fraying.

By far the quickest short cut is to buy one of the countless duvet covers available with printed images on them already – a space scene, a fairytale, woodland animals, for example. All you have to do here is attach tab tops and you have created an instant adventure in less than half an hour.

how to make a doorway puppet theatre

Puppets theatres are rare these days, but are easy to set up and an instant hit with children, who love to perform their favourite fairy stories. They will also welcome new characters that you develop together from scraps of fabric, beads and buttons.

you will need

Striped fabric, approx.
  90 x 120 cm (36 x 48 in)
  (to fit chosen doorway)
Sewing machine and matching
  threads
Tape measure
Tailor's chalk
Contrasting fabric, approx.
  1 m (1 yd) in width
Scissors
Dressmaker's pins
2 ribbon tiebacks, each 30 cm
  (12 in) long
Checked fabric, approx. 50 cm
  (20 in)
Pinking shears
Red tape, approx. 2 m (2 yd)
Drill
2 eyehooks

1) Hem all sides of the striped fabric, which will form the façade of the theatre, allowing 3 cm (1 in) for turnover. Lay the fabric flat and, using tailor's chalk and a tape measure, mark out the 'stage' area. This example is 25 cm (10 in) from the top and 17 cm (6 ¾ in) from each side, to make a stage hole that measures 45 x 40 cm (18 x 16 in).

2) Cut two curtains from the contrasting fabric and hem the sides and bottom. Here, they measure 55 x 25 cm (22 x 10 in). Pin the top edge of the curtain to the back of the stage opening. Pin the ribbon tiebacks in place on either side of the stage.

3) Cut triangles from the checked fabric, using pinking shears. You can sew miniature versions of the ones on page 54 if you prefer. Arrange the triangles and sew them to the top edge of the stage or theatre opening.

4) To frame the stage, pin and stitch the tape around the edges of the stage opening, neatly covering the triangle edges and fastening the curtains and tiebacks in place.

5) To hang the theatre in a doorway, first measure the width of your doorframe. Make two loops of fabric with the remaining red tape and stitch each to one top corner of the puppet theatre and hang from eyehooks screwed into each corner of the frame, pre-drilling the holes.

how to make a sailboat façade

This is the perfect hanging to complete a cosy cabin interior you have set up under the stairs or in some other alcove of the house. Boys and girls will love to dress as pirates or sailors to live the part.

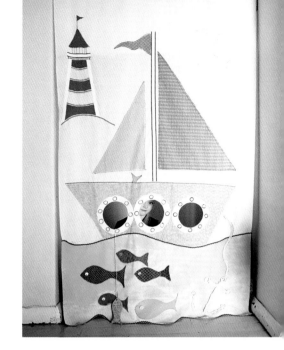

1) Lay the background fabric out flat and draw on your design using tailor's chalk. Decide which areas you are going to paint – the sea, some of the fish, parts of the lighthouse – and paint them in with fabric paint.

2) Use tailor's chalk to draw outlines for all of the fabric shapes you need and cut them out. These might include sails, boat, flag, water, fish, lighthouse and any other details you want to add. Pin, and then sew, the cut-out shapes in position.

3) Cut out a number of portholes: the ideal size is 25 cm (10 in) across. Measure and cut out felt porthole surrounds and glue in place. When dry, draw black rivets on the felt using a fabric pen.

4) Sew a button eye onto each fish. Measure, cut and pin lengths of ribbon for parts of the lighthouse, and for the mast of the lighthouse. Machine-stitch these on. Take a length of rope and arrange it to make an anchor shape. Glue in place.

5) Measure and saw the wooden pole to fit your hanging space. Fold over the top of the background fabric to make a casing wide enough for the pole. Attach a short length of rope to each end of the pole and hang from eyehooks screwed into each corner of the frame, pre-drilling the holes.

you will need

140 x 200 cm (56 x 72 in) background fabric

Tailor's chalk

Fabric paint

Paintbrush

1 m (1 yd) sail fabric

50 cm (20 in) boat fabric

25 cm (10 in) fish fabric

Scissors

Dressmaker's pins

Sewing machine and matching threads

3 squares of coloured felt, approx. 21 cm (8½ in) square each

Fabric glue

Black fabric pen

Buttons

2 m (2 yd) ribbon

2 m (2 yd) rope

Wooden pole

Saw

Drill

2 eyehooks

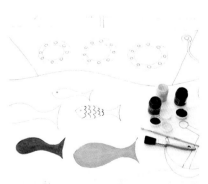

how to make an under-the-table house

Nothing could be easier than draping a large sheet over a table to make a secret play space underneath, which can become anything from a tent in the jungle to a mountaintop castle. This example has a playhouse feel to it.

1) Decide on the height and width of the door and windows needed. Measure and mark up on your sheet with tailor's chalk and cut out.

2) Cut a door 'curtain' from a scrap of fabric using pinking shears and making it 2 cm (¾ in) wider than the doorway. Stitch it to the top of the doorway.

3) Measure and cut out plastic 'windows'. They should be about 4 cm (1½ in) bigger than the window opening. Pin these in place behind the openings and stitch down.

4) Measure and cut four curtains from matching scraps of fabric, using pinking shears. Attach these to the 'outside' of the sheet, carefully stitching them to the house along the top of the window, and taking care to conceal the plastic window seam beneath. Make two fabric tie backs per curtain and stitch in place.

you will need

Large sheet or sheeting fabric to fit over your table
Tape measure
Tailor's chalk
Scissors
Fabric scraps
Pinking shears
Sewing machine and matching thread
Plastic sheeting
Dressmaker's pins

Cut out window box flowers from floral fabric and hand stitch to the 'house' just beneath the window. Or collect beautifully made silk flowers and glue into place.

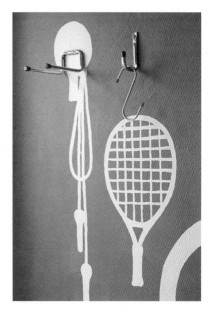
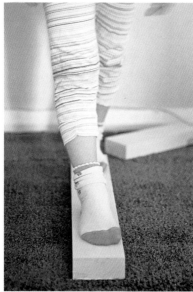

indoor exercise space

Many activities that children enjoy come with paraphernalia, from bicycles to tennis rackets. While this equipment is usually worth having, storing it all can be tricky. Luckily, there are other activities can be rolled up in a bag and taken out and about.

All children need regular, active exercise, whether it be playing football after school, attending weekly dance lessons or spending half an hour in the park. As well as encouraging outdoor activities and sports, make the effort to dedicate areas of your home to active exercise. This could be as basic as **storing equipment for outdoor use** (see page 94). This will encourage your children to use their sports gear far more because it is easily accessible.

You should also devise energetic activities to do indoors come rain, hail or snow. Punch bags, hopscotch mats and skipping ropes work wonders for children who need to burn up energy and can be used in a bedroom or even a passageway. None of them takes up much space and are good value to buy.

If you have the space for a permanent sports area, consider laying down some fake grass. Available from most carpeting shops, this is the perfect base for balancing beams and crawl-through tunnels. Make a few beanbags for children to throw to each other and keep a collection of balls and rackets.

how to store sports equipment

Use a hallway or wall space under the stairs for storing your large sports gear. This gets equipment off the floor and out of the way, while teaching children that everything has a home at the end of the day.

1) Paint your background wall in a basic colour. Decide where you want to hang each piece of sports equipment and screw hooks into pre-drilled holes at appropriate positions on the wall to make sure it all fits nicely.

2) With the equipment in place, use chalk or a pencil to trace and draw the outline of each piece. Remove the equipment and paint the outlines, freehand, using a lighter paint colour.

3) Return everything to its allotted space.

activity spaces

you will need

Acrylic PVA paint
Paintbrush or roller with tray
Drill
Sports equipment hooks
Masonry screws
Rawlplugs
Screwdriver
Chalk or pencil

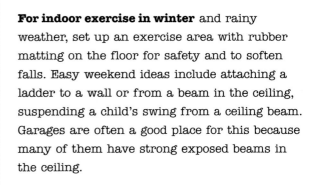

For indoor exercise in winter and rainy weather, set up an exercise area with rubber matting on the floor for safety and to soften falls. Easy weekend ideas include attaching a ladder to a wall or from a beam in the ceiling, suspending a child's swing from a ceiling beam. Garages are often a good place for this because many of them have strong exposed beams in the ceiling.

Keep large chalks handy for children to use to draw outside on paving. They could draw a track for riding bikes on the pavement or hopscotch on the driveway. You can wash it off using a garden hose or wait for it to rain.

95

4 quiet spaces

play tents

Children love the thrill of crawling inside their own little play tent made from sheets and blankets, closing the 'door' and creating their own imaginary world, secure in the knowledge that the space is theirs to enjoy for hours on end.

Play tents can take on many forms, from **teepees** (see page 100) to **hula-hoop fabric tents** (see pages 104–105) to the **garden tent** seen in Chapter 1 (see page 32). The tents are easy to make and can be put up in any area of the home, either temporarily or as a permanent fixture. Both offer a surprisingly compact way of creating a make-believe play space in the home.

Taking up an area the size of a coffee table but easy to move, these play tents double as travelling play spaces so that you can keep an eye your children while cooking, working or doing homework

with an older child. They are great in bedrooms, too – at the foot of the bed or in a corner, where you can encourage fantasy play. Add a soft rug or duvet on the floor to make it warm and cosy. Provide torches for shadow play and 'midnight' feasts (draw the curtains and pretend it's night time), or set up a picnic or tea party. Your instant 'house' will have been transformed as your children gather up their favourite toys and haul them inside. Friends will discover it in no time, more role-playing will be invented, and little people will be kept busy for hours.

you will need

240 cm (8 ft) x 150 cm (5 ft)
   fabric, approx.
Long ruler or tape measure
Pencil
Pinking shears or scissors
Dressmaker's pins
Sewing machine and matching
   thread
50 cm (20 in) flat elastic,
   1 cm (¼ in) wide
5 wooden poles, approx.
   160 cm (68 in) long
100 cm (40 in) thin rope or
   twine

how to make a teepee

Not only a rainy-day standby, this easy-to-assemble
teepee has other uses too: it can be set up indoors or
out (very popular at parties) and even taken away
on holiday or to the beach in the summer.

1) Lay out your fabric on a
flat surface. Using a long ruler
or tape measure and a pencil,
mark 80 cm (32 in) intervals
along one long edge, starting
at the left-hand side of the
fabric. Along the opposite long
edge measure 40 cm (16 in)
in from the left-hand side and
make a mark. From here,
measure and mark 80 cm
(32 in) intervals as before.

2) With the pencil and long
ruler or tape measure as a
guide, join these marks to
make a zigzag across the
fabric. This will give you four
elongated triangles, each with
an 80 cm (32 in) base, plus

two right-angled triangles,
each with a 40 cm (16 in)
base. See below.

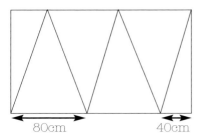

3) Cut out the triangles using
pinking shears, and trim
7.5 cm (3 in) off the pointed
top of each one. Pin the longest
sides of the triangles together
in turn, lining them up at the
base, and with one right-angled
triangle at each end. Make sure

you place the right sides of the fabric together. The pinned result is now a curved piece of fabric. See below.

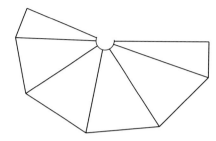

4) Sew the seams leaving a 1.5 cm (⅝ in) seam allowance. Zigzag stitch the raw edges if necessary to prevent fraying. Bring the right sides of the right-angled triangles together, and sew a 20 cm (8 in) seam from the top edge downwards. Hem the remaining raw edges to create a neat finish.

5) Next, make five elastic loops to secure the fabric to the poles. Cut the elastic into five equal lengths, and stitch the ends of each length to the fabric of the seam allowance of each seam, approximately 10 cm (4 in) up from the bottom hem.

6) Line one wooden pole up with each of the teepee seams, placing them inside the elastic loops. Stand the teepee up and, using the thin rope, tie the poles together at the top, winding the rope in between and around the poles to restrict their movement. To store your tepee, simply untie the top, fold up and stash away in a cupboard for the next play day.

Create a window by cutting four squares out of one panel, and if you have time, add a little curtain flap. Use combinations of stripes, florals, spots or checks or you can simply create your panels in plain fabric or sheeting and have fun decorating it afterwards.

You can all have fun adding streamers or decorating the teepee with ribbons, fabric glitter glue or paint, potato prints and even handprints. Attach triangles of leftover fabric to string and drape them around the poles or string them up in the garden for added colour and fun.

how to make a hula-hoop fabric tent

This tent is easy to make out of a bed sheet and such fun to decorate. Opt for a fairy-castle or medieval-turret theme to encourage fantasy play and furnish with mats, cushions and anything soft to sit on.

you will need

Bed sheet, 230 x 260 cm (90 x 100 in) approx., or similar

Tape measure

Sewing machine and matching thread

Large safety pin

Soft string for drawstring, 1 cm (½ in) thick

Cane hoop, approx. 65 cm (26 in) diameter

4 equal lengths string or ribbon, approx. 50 cm (20 in) each

Cup hook

1) Lay out the bed sheet and fold over the top (short) edge by 10 cm (4 in) to make a neat casing for the drawstring. You can adapt the width of your casing to fit any drawstring, but make sure that the string can move freely once inside the casing so that it draws up easily. Iron the casing flat and stitch along the raw edge.

2) The beauty of using a ready-made sheet is that it is hemmed already and saves time. If you are using an alternative fabric, however, hem the two sides and the base, allowing approximately 8 cm (3 in) all around, so that it hangs neatly when finished.

3) Attach a safety pin to one end of the drawstring and thread through the casing. Set aside. Tie the four lengths of string or ribbon to the hula-hoop at equal distances from each other. (See below.) Gather the loose ends together in the centre of the hoop and knot together securely. Fix onto the hook.

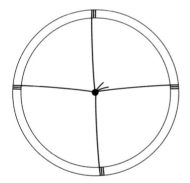

4) Pull up the drawstring on the tent, leaving a circle of about 20 cm (8 in) in the centre, and arrange the sheet over the hoop until it fits neatly. The easiest way to do this is to pick up the hook with one hand (with the hoop suspended by the four ribbons or strings beneath it) and adjust the fabric using your other hand. Let the tent swing around until the opening or 'door' faces the right direction.

5) Screw the cup hook into the ceiling. Attach the hula-hoop tent and rearrange the drawstring so that it hangs neatly.

Decorate a hula-hoop tent with fabric paint, felt shapes, buttons, shells and literally anything that takes your fancy. Let your children get creative with their own decorations and they'll be busy for hours.

Stitch pockets onto the outside (or inside) to provide storage for soft toys, books, games, dolls' clothes or anything else that is needed for play.

Cut windows into the fabric 'walls' – round porthole shapes, square ones or tall thin ones for imaginary castles all work well. The trick is to keep them quite small so that they don't make the fabric gape or sag.

Stitch ribbons on either side of the door opening so that it can be tied shut for privacy or to keep the light out.

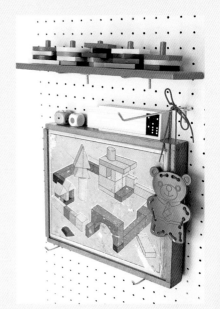
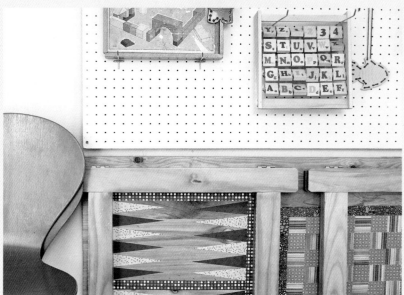

games area

An activity area, complete with games table, provides
the perfect flat surface for doing art, making puzzles
or playing board games. Different activities can be left
for days on end without being disturbed or damaged.

It is always a challenge to keep puzzle
pieces together and to maintain interest
in board games, so this activity space
creates an environment where
everything can be stored in its own
place and seen at a glance, which means
that expensive games are enjoyed more
often. Used as a workbench, the **games
table** is the focus of this area and is also
great for science experiments,
woodwork creations, or for papier-
mâché, clay and sewing. Electric train
sets also need a dust-free place to be set
up and admired and an activity table is
an ideal alternative to the floor.

You can set up an activity area at the
end of a hallway or in the corner of

the kitchen, or even in an outside
garage area. If space is limited, you
can fold the table against a wall when
it's not being used. Make full use of
the wall above the table by attaching
a peg board with hooks for shelves,
storage tins and games so that you
can hang everything up neatly and
out of the way of little fingers. Move
the pegs around as new tins and
boxes need to be stored. You can hang
absolutely anything of any shape or
size. As well as buying games to play,
you can make a few of your own,
incorporating them into novel designs,
such as the **snakes and ladders
tablecloth** (see page 109).

how to make a games table

These work best if made on the top of a trestle table. You can incorporate any board games into your design, either painted or made with paper. Decorate one side with découpage if it is going to be used for sewing or clay modelling.

1) Draw your board-game patterns onto the tabletop in pencil, using a ruler to measure and check against your design for accuracy. Cut the board-game pieces from scrapbooking paper and glue in place.

2) Once the layout is complete, varnish with two coats, leaving the first coat to dry thoroughly before starting the second. For an absolutely smooth finish, give the table a light sand before applying the second coat. (Alternatively, paint the board-game shapes with acrylic paint, using masking tape to help keep the lines straight.)

3) This table is attached to the wall and folds down when not in use. Screw the two heavy-duty hinges to one long edge of the table. Now make a rope handle. Drill two holes through the table, at the centre of the opposite long edge of the table, thread the rope through and knot on both sides. This makes it easier to pull the tabletop up for use. Finally, screw the tabletop in position on the wall.

you will need

Trestle table

Pencil

Ruler

Scrapbooking paper

Scissors

All-purpose glue

Varnish

Sandpaper

Drill

2 heavy-duty hinges with screws

Screwdriver

Short length of rope

how to make a snakes and ladders tablecloth

Use checked fabric to make the squares for a game of snakes and ladders and find a large die and playing pieces. Sewing the board at the centre of a large sheet gives children something to sit on when playing outdoors.

1) Use tailor's chalk to mark the outline of play on the checked fabric, starting in the bottom left-hand corner. This example uses 11 x 13 squares and measures 57 x 64 cm (22½ x 25 in). Each square is 5 cm (2 in) square.

2) Set your sewing machine to satin stitch, and stitch the outline onto the fabric in contrasting thread, using the tailor's chalk as a guide. Using a fabric pen, number each square, working from the left to right in the bottom row, right to left in the next, and so on, to show the direction of play.

3) Cut out four felt snakes. The length of each will depend on which squares you wish to join. Make some long and some short. Make four ladders from the ribbon, again varying the length. Position the snakes and ladders on the 'board' and stitch them onto the fabric.

4) Trim the edges of the checked fabric, turn under and sew onto a large sheet of fabric that protects the table.

you will need

Tailor's chalk
Checked fabric (you need at
  least 36 squares)
Sewing machine and
  contrasting thread
Fabric pen
Large felt square
Scissors
Narrow ribbon approx. 200 cm
  (80 in)
Bed sheet, approx.
  230 x 260 cm (90 x 100 in),
  or similar

To make metal storage tins, recycle biscuit tins by painting them and use them to store puzzle pieces, game pieces, dice or dominoes.

A trestle table is easy to fold out or put away and can be useful for family entertaining or children's parties. Set the table up on grass in summer with a protective plastic fabric cloth over it and use for party food, or for messy projects such as clay-modelling and painting.

homework space

Homework spaces need to be attractive as well as practical. The easiest way to keep everything organized is to create enough storage for books and stationery as well as a useful work surface and accessible pin board.

Workspace units made from modular pieces are easy to move around a bedroom or study (see page 112). Once you child grows out of it, you can recycle the different pieces to make another storage unit for a different child, such as the foldaway cupboard in Chapter 3 or even shelving. Use the same principle to make a larger desk for two children to share or a smaller one to fit under a bunk bed.

Work together with your child on this project so that they enjoy sitting in the space and feels comfortable doing their homework there. Decorate the area with a wall stencil, add an adjustable anglepoise lamp and seek out some comfortable seating.

You can personalize the space by adding a **pretty pin board** from an artist's canvas, a magnetic board or cork tiles (see page 113). Encourage your child to hang art, drawings, jewellery and precious items, so that the space becomes a mirror image of her interests and special memories.

how to make a basic workspace unit

This is a very basic desk design, put together with ready-made boxes (available from most large hardware stores). Be as creative as you like and enjoy making it with your children, allowing them to help with the painting.

you will need

Four ready-made boxes
Tape measure
Length of wood for desktop
Satin-sheen paint
Paintbrush
Drill
Screws
Screwdriver
Wood filler

1) You are going to stack the boxes in pairs and rest the desktop on top, leaving enough space between them to tuck in a chair – approximately 150 cm (60 in). Add this measurement to the width of two boxes to calculate the length of desktop that you need.

2) Paint the boxes using a scheme that suits the décor. You can edge the boxes in a single colour or paint the walls different colours – it is up to you. While the paint is drying, paint the desktop. Leave everything to dry overnight.

3) To construct the workspace unit, simply stack the boxes in pairs and use these to support the desktop. Screw down the top for extra stability, pre-drilling the holes, countersinking the screws and covering the screw heads with wood filler. Touch up with paint.

Use pretty stencils to decorate the wall. Letters of the alphabet and numbers are great educational aids, helping to create a complete learning-focused environment. Paint them in a muted colour so that they don't clash with the rest of the décor.

how to make a pretty pin board

Pin boards are ideal 'mood' boards that function as useful places to pin school timetables and reminders, but also to decorate with favourite things that make a child feel happy when they look at it.

1) Place your board on the floor. Use lengths of pretty ribbon to create a border, fixing it in place with drawing pins or using a staple gun. This not only finishes off the board neatly, but provides a place for tucking in photos or invitations. Repeat the ribbon idea across the board in parallel lines or criss-crossing them for a different effect.

you will need

Painting canvas or any pin board to fit your space
Collection of pretty ribbons
Drawing pins or staple gun

Set up a wonderfully efficient system of clipboards. Simply add a dado rail clip to the top of the clipboard and hang. Each one can represent a different day of the week, with all the activities listed or identified by a fun symbol – for example: a triangle for music, goggles for swimming or a painting for art. Children can understand these symbols and will soon become responsible for their own activities.

water space

Water play is one of the most enjoyable educational activities for children and doesn't need to be restricted to bath time. The more messy the better, of course, so it's perfect for hot days when the kids need to cool off. But there are plenty of fun indoor water-play activities.

Playing with colour Set up two or three water basins on a table and carefully add a different food colouring to each one. Let children mix it slowly and watch as it makes fascinating patterns. Once mixed, add colours together to make new ones.

Catching fish Watch as your children master their hand-eye coordination when trying to hook a fish. Provide a bucket for their catch and count them together at the end.

Making fish Cut fish shapes from colourful plastic file dividers. Make a hole for an eye with a punch, then thread a metal paperclip through it and drop it into a basin of water. Fishing rods are easily constructed from a pole and a length of string with a magnet fastened securely onto the end.

Pouring and filling Place a bowl on a low table and provide plenty of plastic cups, spoons and bowls and later move on to sponges, eggbeaters and anything that the children fancy from your baking drawer. Older children will love plastic syringes to squirt water, as well as measuring spoons and funnels. It's worth keeping certain items from the sea of plastic that kids accumulate over the years for playtimes such as these.

Washing clothes Washing dolls' clothes can give hours of joy. Lots of bubbles add to the fun and hanging it all up with pegs is a good exercise in motor coordination. Set up a string washing line between two chairs (this also works well in the garden), or hang one at the right height over the bath so that the clothes don't drip on the floor.

Paper boat races Make boats from squares of paper and let the children colour their own so that they can identify them. Have some fun racing the boats in a large basin of water, encouraging the children to blow them along or ripple the water to make waves. Be prepared for lots of splashing.

Making bubbles Blow down straws or a soft pipe into water to make bubbles and strange noises. Add bubble bath or dishwashing liquid and let kids mix it into a bubbly froth with an eggbeater.

cosy corner

This does not have to be a permanent feature in a room, but can be set up in the winter months to create a cosy spot with plenty of sunlight for reading and relaxing in the warmth.

This is simply a collection of comfy mattresses and cushions that create an inviting den for a weekend, a week or longer. Choose fabrics and colours that will give it a quiet energy and create the feeling of a library with plenty of books and even a comfy armchair or **lounger** (see page 121).

This is a great project to do with your children. Choose the cushions with them and let them make the decorative snowflakes for the windows.

Window seats are ideal for alcoves but you can easily create one even if your windows are from ceiling to floor (see page 118). If not, a simple bench and cushions work well too. Depending on the space you have available, you might even throw in a personalized **beanbag** or two (see page 120).

how to make a cosy window seat

Transform a corner of a sunny room with this cosy window seat – quite simply a single mattress covered in hardwearing fabric. Throw in a couple scatter cushions to fully indulge your child's love of lounging around.

1) Cover the mattress in durable upholstery fabric, making sure it is easy to remove and fully washable.

2) Make an outsized 'headboard' using two square cushions tied together or one larger, covered cushion.

3) Add a fluffy cushion or two, and some storage crates to use as tables and to keep the place tidy at the end of the day.

you will need
Single mattress
Upholstery fabric
A mix of cushions
Storage crates

quiet spaces

Window snowflakes keep children busy for hours. Use bond paper or tissue paper, fold into four and cut a quarter-circle shape while holding the corner in your hand. Open the circle out flat on a table and fold again – first in half, then in quarters, and finally in eighths. Cut patterns along the edges of the folds and unfold carefully, taking care not to tear the paper. You will have created a patterned snowflake. Tack to the window, make some more to go with it and enjoy!

Storage is vital in these cosy corners. Use wine crates or any wooden boxes, paint them bold colours and use them for storing books, CDs or extra blankets.

how to personalize a beanbag

A beanbag makes a wonderfully flexible addition to any space, and can be used all over the house. Personalize it by adding your child's name and they will use it for reading in their bedroom or beside a low table as an extra chair.

1) Follow the diagram to cut the following pieces from the denim fabric: four side panels, one pocket, one circle for the top and one circle for the bottom, cut in half (see below).

2) Edge the pocket and pin it 18 cm (7 in) up from the base of one of the panels. Stitch in place.

3) Decide on the size of letters for your child's name. You can draw these freehand on paper or type the name into a computer and play around with sizes before printing out to use as a template.

4) Iron appliqué paper to the back of a scrap of fabric large enough for your child's name. Pin your printed template to the front and cut out the letters carefully. Peel off the bottom layer of appliqué paper, and place the letters 25 cm (10 in) from the bottom of the second panel. Iron on and sew around each letter using satin stitch. Iron again.

5) Pin and sew the four side panels together; pin and stitch the small circle into the top of the bag. Pin and sew the large circle pieces (right sides together) to the base of the bag leaving an 8 cm (3 in) gap in the centre seam for the stuffing.

6) Fill the bag three-quarters full with polystyrene beads and sew up the opening.

quiet spaces

you will need

150 cm (60 inches) square denim fabric

Tape measure

Tailor's chalk

Scissors

Sewing machine and matching thread

Dressmaker's pins

Fabric scraps

Double-sided appliqué paper (enough for child's name)

3 kg (6½ lb) polystyrene beads

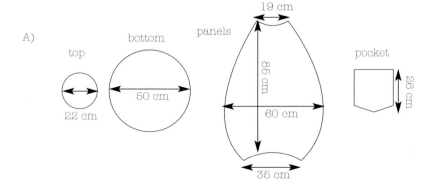

A)

top 22 cm

bottom 50 cm

panels 19 cm 85 cm 60 cm 35 cm

pocket 26 cm

how to make a comfy lounger

This lounger provides the perfect soft area for reading and doing projects on the floor – something children love to do. Scatter cushions are a space-saving alternative to a mattress, as they are easier to move and store.

1) To make the ties, cut four 28 cm (11 in) lengths of tape per cushion. Hand-stitch one tie to each corner of a cushion. Tie the cushions together to make a 'bed' of two cushions by four.

2) To make a futon-style lounger, position the cushions so that the top four fold up against a wall for the back of the futon, and the bottom four fold up against the floor for the seat.

you will need
8 large square cushions
900 cm (354 in) tape to match
Scissors
Needle and matching thread

These scatter cushions can also be tied into a bed shape for small children and then untied and used on chairs or stacked and stored in a cupboard when not in use.

templates

100%
page 56

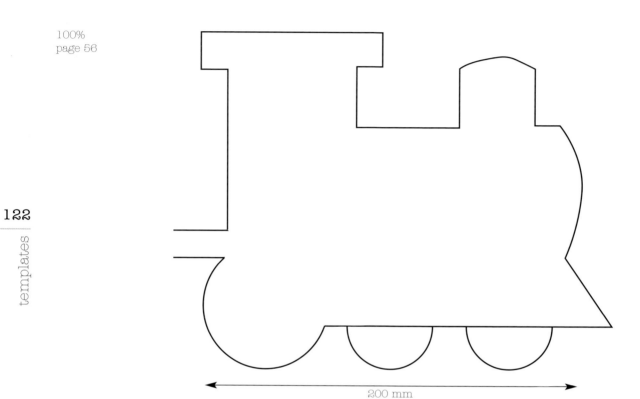

200 mm

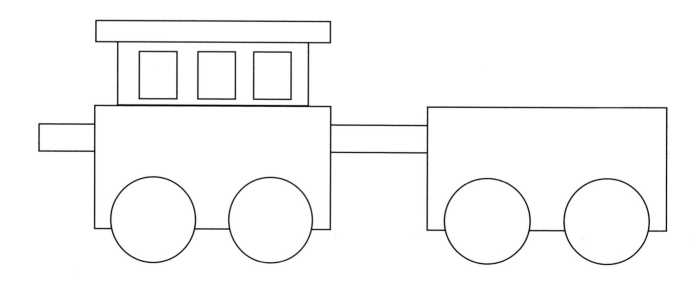

100%
page 64

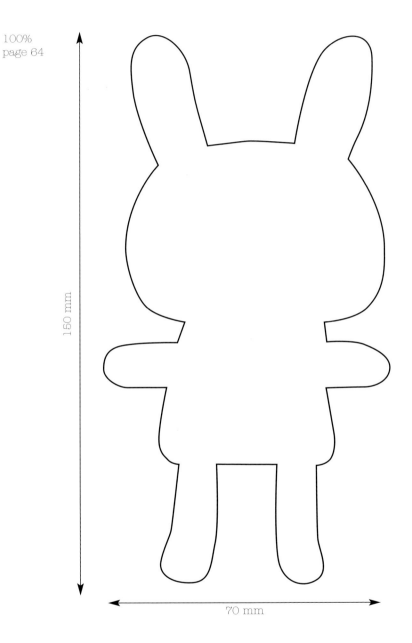

150 mm

70 mm

templates

100%
page 15

150 mm

400 mm

100%

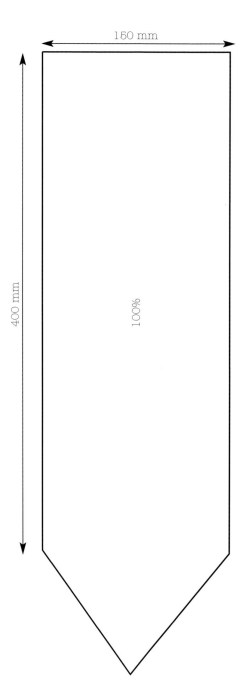

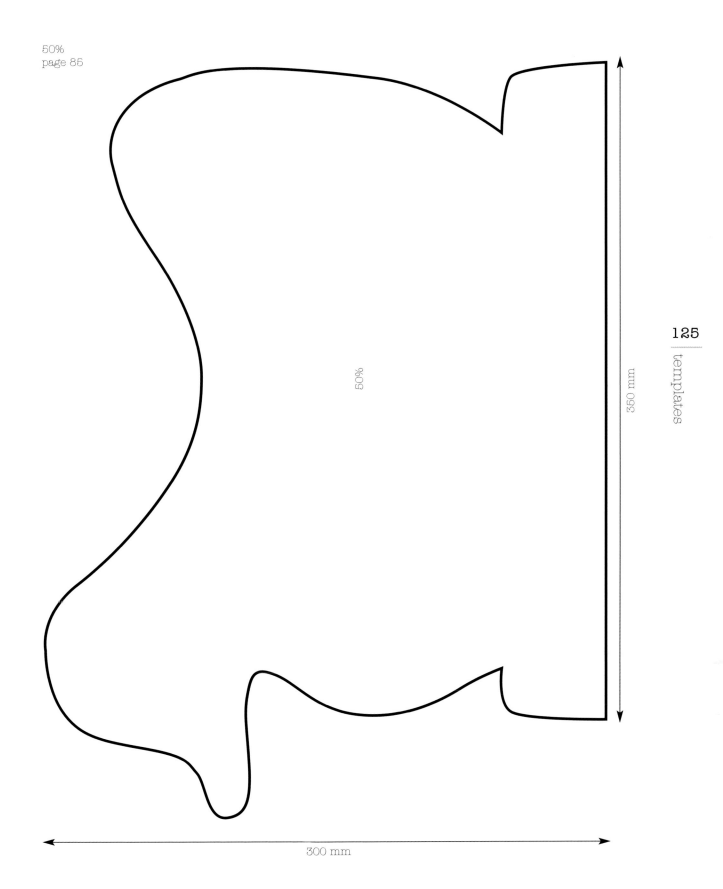

50%

350 mm

300 mm

index

index

acknowledgements

Many thanks to Katy Denny of Hamlyn who took a leap of faith in all my creative abilities. My book has been produced after just one meeting with her and many transatlantic emails! Also to her team who have designed a very beautiful book.

I am very grateful to my friends and their families who allowed me to shoot in their homes and personal spaces. I would not have been able to capture the essence of these play spaces in this book without the amazing children playing in them.

Thanks to Lindsay Nagel for her wonderful garden, her children Sandra and Ross, and their friends Miles, Luke and Rosanna. Nicola Lapid and her daughter Ruby and Rosita Roberts for the tree house shoots and Dennis Buckland for swinging in the tree. Lauren Bauer for her shop wall where I did the wall mural, her lovely house and children Ben and Ella who were great little models. Noeleen van der Leek for Alexander and Julia and their musical smiles, Robyn Snyman for Aiden's and the teepee pictures, Colleen Doyle for her playroom and daughters Bianca and Julia. Alex and Troy, Elihle, Ayla, Noah, Jordan and his sister Kirsty for enjoying playing in my pictures! Thanks to Annette and Judith who helped renovate the magical play cupboard.

And thanks to my daughter Georgia, who obviously appears many times in my book, who is my life, my inspiration, my boss and my imagination.

To my favourite photographers, Warren Heath, Anton de Beer and Brooke Fasani who helped capture my ideas. Warren, who is a new dad himself and who did most of the pictures, was able to really capture the playfulness of each child with such lovely lighting.

To Michelle Snaddon who wrote the inspiring words to all of my ideas, explaining in fine detail how to make and put together every play space. Her practical knowledge and input was invaluable. Michelle's been involved in book publishing and decor magazines for 15 years, has two beautiful children of her own and is the same kind of creative mother as me!

And, last but not least, to my mother Annette who helped me design, sew, paint, stitch and glue absolutely every idea together in this book, and a bigger thanks for assisting me on all of the shoots - it was a lot of hard work but worth every minute, resulting in the most inspiring pictures for my book.

www.samscarborough.com

SPECIAL PHOTOGRAPHY

© Octopus Publishing Group Limited/Anton de Beer 10, 16-21, 24-34, 46 bottom, 47 top and middle, 55 bottom, 58-60, 70 top, 78, 80, 86 middle, 88 bottom, 95 bottom, 104, 105, 108 right, 109 left; /Brooke Fasani 1-3, 7, 22-23, 42-45, 49, 97-103, 114; /Warren Heath 4, 5, 11-15, 36-41, 46 top and middle, 47 bottom, 48, 50-54, 55 top, 56-57, 61-67, 70 middle and right, 71-77, 79, 81-85, 86 left and right, 88 top, 89-94, 95 top, 106-107, 108 top and left, 109 top, 110-113, 116-121.

Executive editor Katy Denny
Editor Ruth Wiseall
Deputy creative director Karen Sawyer
Designer Joanna MacGregor
Production controller Amanda Mackie